READING AND WRITING
JAPANESE
HIRAGANA

A Character Workbook for Beginners

EMIKO KONOMI

Illustrated by Jessica Anecito

TUTTLE Publishing

Tokyo | Rutland, Vermont | Singapore

"Books to Span the East and West"

Tuttle Publishing was founded in 1832 in the small New England town of Rutland, Vermont [USA]. Our core values remain as strong today as they were then—to publish best-in-class books which bring people together one page at a time. In 1948, we established a publishing office in Japan—and Tuttle is now a leader in publishing English-language books about the arts, languages and cultures of Asia. The world has become a much smaller place today and Asia's economic and cultural influence has grown. Yet the need for meaningful dialogue and information about this diverse region has never been greater. Over the past seven decades, Tuttle has published thousands of books on subjects ranging from martial arts and paper crafts to language learning and literature—and our talented authors, illustrators, designers and photographers have won many prestigious awards. We welcome you to explore the wealth of information available on Asia at **www.tuttlepublishing.com**.

Published by Tuttle Publishing, an imprint of Periplus Editions (HK) Ltd.

www.tuttlepublishing.com

Copyright © 2019 by Periplus Editions (HK) Ltd.
Illustration page 83 by hermandesign 2015.

ISBN: 978-4-8053-1521-7

Distributed by:

North America, Latin America & Europe
Tuttle Publishing
364 Innovation Drive
North Clarendon, VT 05759-9436 U.S.A.
Tel: 1 (802) 773-8930
Fax: 1 (802) 773-6993
info@tuttlepublishing.com
www.tuttlepublishing.com

Asia Pacific
Berkeley Books Pte. Ltd.
3 Kallang Sector #04-01
Singapore 349278
Tel: (65) 6741-2178
Fax: (65) 6741-2179
inquiries@periplus.com.sg
www.tuttlepublishing.com

Japan
Tuttle Publishing
Yaekari Building, 3rd Floor
5-4-12 Osaki
Shinagawa-ku
Tokyo 141 0032
Tel: (81) 3 5437-0171
Fax: (81) 3 5437-0755
sales@tuttle.co.jp
www.tuttle.co.jp

First edition
25 24 23 22   8 7 6 5 4
Printed in Malaysia   2112VP

TUTTLE PUBLISHING® is a registered trademark of Tuttle Publishing, a division of Periplus Editions (HK) Ltd.

CONTENTS

PART 1

Reading and Writing Hiragana: The Basics

PART 2

Reading and Writing Hiragana: Vocabulary Practice

How to Use This Book

Who is this book for?

The book is primarily designed for learners of Japanese who wish to master the reading and writing of *hiragana*, one of the three fundamental scripts of the Japanese language, the others being *katakana* and *kanji* (see page 6). The book is aimed at beginning-level students and no knowledge of Japanese grammar is required.

When Japanese children are first learning to read and write, they learn the hiragana script before the katakana script. Once you have mastered the hiragana in this book, I recommend learning katakana, using this book's companion title *Reading and Writing Japanese Katakana*.

What is the purpose of this book?

The purpose of this book is to introduce the symbols of the hiragana script and to provide ample practice material to promote practical competence in reading and writing.

Hiragana symbols are introduced using plentiful sample words and expressions chosen for their common practical usage in contemporary Japan. They are selected for their utility in discussing subjects relevant to modern adult Japanese speakers. Learners will have abundant opportunity to practice through realistic drills and exercises.

How is this book structured?

This book is comprised of two chapters. The first chapter introduces the stroke order of each hiragana symbol, along with basic reading and writing practice. The second chapter presents common and practical hiragana vocabulary grouped into subject categories. Ample practice material is provided for each category. Drills and exercises are organized in a manner that ensures systematic progress. Online audio files recorded by native Japanese speakers are available on the Tuttle website (see address at the bottom of the facing page). These are an excellent tool for learning the "sound-to-symbol" connection, and for hearing new vocabulary words used in an authentic context.

How is hiragana presented in this book?

Each symbol is first separately introduced following the traditional Japanese order. Grid-like boxes are provided to help learners write symbols with the correct stroke order, relative positioning and uniform size. Once learners are comfortable writing an individual symbol, they progress to practice writing that symbol within frequently used words that include it, rather than practice writing in isolation. The goal of reading and writing Japanese is not to merely recognize and write individual symbols, but rather to understand authentic texts. This book is designed to help learners achieve this goal.

Study tips

- Progress in order: each section is built upon preceding sections. Do not skip around.
- Practice mindfully: avoid mindless copying or tracing. Test your memory.
- Cover the model examples and see if you can reproduce the symbols on your own.
- Download the free flashcards from this book's website at the link below to help you memorize the symbols.
- Once you have mastered the symbols, practice them in meaningful units of vocabulary rather than in isolation
- Do the Reading and Writing Practice exercises in Part 2 in order: each exercise is built on preceding exercises.
- Download gridded writing sheets from this book's website for further handwriting practice.
- Use the online audio files at the address below for sound-symbol connection
- Frequently revisit old material ("loop back")

Repetition is key in learning a language. It improves memory and fluency, builds up confidence, and helps with application. Set a learning schedule and stick to it to form good habits. Frequently revisit previously studied material. I suggest that after covering three symbols, you loop back to the first two before moving on to the fourth. Once you are comfortable with five individual symbols, move beyond isolated symbols and practice reading them in meaningful words as soon as possible. You can choose your own pace at which to work, but make sure you loop back frequently.

Ideally, users of this book will have already learned some of the spoken language, in line with the principles of language acquisition, in which development of the listening and speaking skills precedes learning how to read and write. But students not yet very familiar with spoken Japanese can use the online audio files to familiarize themselves with native Japanese pronunciation of each symbol as it is introduced. As you study each symbol and sample words, listen, repeat, and listen again. Saying the words out loud helps you learn them, as well as polishing your Japanese pronunciation, so don't be shy about it.

Moving on

Students who have mastered the exercises in this book, and students who already have a working knowledge of Japanese grammar can build on their skills with further study materials that can be found on this book's online site. The audio files used in the book can also be accessed here, along with gridded paper for handwriting practice, and downloadable flashcards. Go to **www.tuttlepublishing.com/reading-and-writing-japanese-katakana**

An Introduction to Hiragana

The Japanese writing system

The modern Japanese writing system combines three types of scripts: *kanji*, *hiragana*, and *katakana*. Kanji characters were originally borrowed from Chinese and adapted to fit Japanese. There are several thousand kanji and Japanese students are required to learn more than two thousand by the time they graduate from high school. Each kanji possesses multiple meanings and can have several pronunciations.

Hiragana and katakana are syllabaries. Each symbol represents one syllabic unit of Japanese but possesses no inherent meaning. The hiragana and katakana syllabaries are comprised of 46 basic symbols, 25 symbols with diacritics, 33 contracted combinations, and some special representations. Whether a word should be written in kanji or hiragana is a matter of convention, although there is room for style. In general, the convention is as follows:

- *Kanji* is used to represent content words (verbs, nouns, adjectives, etc.) or parts of content words.
- *Hiragana* is used to write function elements such as grammatical endings and particles, and words for which there is no commonly accepted kanji.
- *Katakana* is used to represent foreign names, loanwords, and onomatopoeia. It is also used for emphasis, or to represent Japanese spoken with unusual accents or a synthesized voice.

Written Japanese sentences combine kanji, hiragana and katakana in highly conventionalized ways to function as a comprehensive writing system. In addition, English alphabet letters and Arabic numerals may be mixed in too, as shown in this example:

デパートは、約 200m 先 です。

(bold = katakana; underlined = hiragana; ☐ = *kanji*)

The department store is about 200 meters ahead.

What is written in hiragana?

As mentioned above, hiragana is used to write function elements, such as grammatical endings and particles, as well as words for which there is no accepted kanji. A person's proficiency in kanji is often associated with his or her educational and intellectual level. While it is possible to use hiragana to write anything in Japanese, native Japanese speakers, even children with a minimal amount of schooling, do not ordinarily write long strings of words in hiragana. However, it is becoming more common these days to see things written all in hiragana due to recent changes in communication.

There are two main changes. One is the increased use of *furigana*, a convention to assist readers with the pronunciation of kanji by providing hiragana placed above the kanji word in horizontal writing, or on the right side in vertical writing. As more foreigners visit or live in

Japan in recent years, furigana is becoming more common, along with romanization and English translation. Another change is due to the popularity of texting as a communication method. Even those words that are traditionally in kanji are now often written in hiragana in text messages.

Under these circumstances, it is important for learners to practice reading and write hiragana beyond the traditional limits. This book provides substantial practice material in this regard.

Vertical and horizontal writing

Modern Japanese can be written horizontally, from left to right, or vertically, from top to bottom starting from the right column and moving left. Due to editorial limitations, text is presented only horizontally in this book. Learners are encouraged to practice vertical writing and develop familiarity with it.

Japanese syllables

The system of *kana*, the collective term for hiragana and katakana, is based on syllables, the basic sound units in Japanese. All Japanese words are made up of syllables that consist of one of the following:

1. A vowel (5 vowels: **a, i, u, e, o**)
2. A consonant plus a vowel (14 consonants; 62 combinations). Note the following special cases:

    /**s+i**/ is pronounced /**shi**/
    /**z+i**/ is pronounced /**ji**/
    /**t+i**/ is pronounced /**chi**/
    /**t+u**/ is pronounced /**tsu**/
    /**d+i**/ is pronounced /**ji**/
    /**d+u**/ is pronounced /**zu**/

3. The syllabic /**n**/. A single /**n**/ makes a full syllable.
4. A long vowel. When a vowel is lengthened to take up two full beats, it is called a long vowel and is presented with a bar on top in this book. There are five long vowels in Japanese:

    aa → ā   **ii → ī**   **uu → ū**   **ee → ē**   **oo** or **ou → ō**

5. A long consonant. A small っ (tsu) before a consonant has the effect of doubling that consonant.
6. A contracted sound: a consonant + /**y**/ + vowel (33 combinations).

The basic 46 hiragana symbols

Japanese syllables are organized in the chart on the next page, which is called the **gojūon-hyō**, meaning "the table of 50 sounds." This fixed order of syllables is used to organize dictionaries and other lists, similar to "alphabetical order" in English. The chart is ten columns wide and five rows high, it thus has 50 blocks. However, since not all blocks are filled, and the syllabic /**n**/ is extra, there are 46 basic syllables. The traditional chart used in Japanese schools is read from right to left, with the **a**, **i**, **u**, **e**, **o** row on the right-hand side of the chart. In this book the chart has been reversed for the benefit of Western readers, and should be read from top to bottom, left to right.

The Basic Hiragana Chart (46 Kana) 🎧 Track 01

	k	s	t	n	h	m	y	r	w	n
あ a	か ka	さ sa	た ta	な na	は ha	ま ma	や ya	ら ra	わ wa	ん n
い i	き ki	し shi	ち chi	に ni	ひ hi	み mi		り ri		
う u	く ku	す su	つ tsu	ぬ nu	ふ fu	む mu	ゆ yu	る ru		
え e	け ke	せ se	て te	ね ne	へ he	め me		れ re		
お o	こ ko	そ so	と to	の no	ほ ho	も mo	よ yo	ろ ro	を o	

Voiced sounds 🎧 Track 02

Diacritical marks can be added to certain unvoiced syllables to indicate voiced or hardened sounds, known as **dakuon** in Japanese.

	g	z	d	b	p
a	が ga	ざ za	だ da	ば ba	ぱ pa
i	ぎ gi	じ ji	ぢ ji	び bi	ぴ pi
u	ぐ gu	ず zu	づ zu	ぶ bu	ぷ pu
e	げ ge	ぜ ze	で de	べ be	ぺ pe
o	ご go	ぞ zo	ど do	ぼ bo	ぽ po

Contracted sounds 🎧 Track 03

There are 33 syllables that can be combined with /**ya**/, /**yu**/ or /**yo**/ to make contracted sounds, known as **yō-on** in Japanese. For example, /**ki**/ and /**ya**/ can be combined to make one syllable, /**kya**/. Note in the chart below that the second syllable is written smaller, to indicate the combination. If the two syllables are the same size then they are treated as uncombined syllables, with the pronunciation of each given equal weight.

	ki	gi	shi	ji	chi	ni	hi	bi	pi	mi	ri
ya	kya きゃ	gya ぎゃ	sha しゃ	ja じゃ	cha ちゃ	nya にゃ	hya ひゃ	bya びゃ	pya ぴゃ	mya みゃ	rya りゃ
yu	kyu きゅ	gyu ぎゅ	shu しゅ	ju じゅ	chu ちゅ	nyu にゅ	hyu ひゅ	byu びゅ	pyu ぴゅ	myu みゅ	ryu りゅ
yo	kyo きょ	gyo ぎょ	sho しょ	jo じょ	cho ちょ	nyo にょ	hyo ひょ	byo びょ	pyo ぴょ	myo みょ	ryo りょ

When written vertically, the small や、ゆ、and よ go in the top right corner. When written horizontally, they go in the bottom left corner.

Long consonants

When the consonants /**t**/, /**s**/, /**k**/, and /**p**/ constitute an entire syllable without a vowel, they are silent, and this lasts a full syllable length. Thus, they are called long consonants, *soku-on* in Japanese. In writing, long consonants are indicated by a small /**tsu**/ っ before the consonant to be lengthened. Compare this with the regular size, つ.

kitto	"surely"	three syllables	**ki-t-to**	きっと
zasshi	"magazine"	three syllabes	**za-s-shi**	ざっし
kekkon	"marriage"	four syllables	**ke-k-ko-n**	けっこん
sapporo	"Sapporo"	four syllables	**sa-p-po-ro**	さっぽろ
massugu	"straight"	four syllables	**ma-s-su-gu**	まっすぐ

When written vertically, the small /**tsu**/ っ goes in the top right corner of a block. When written horizontally, it goes in the bottom left corner.

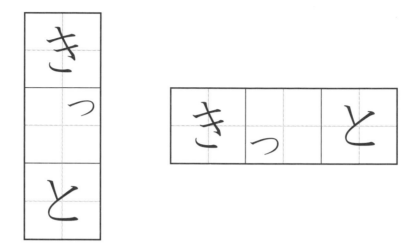

Punctuation

Two Japanese punctuation marks are introduced in this book.

。 This marks the end of a sentence like the period marks the end of an English sentence. In Japanese this is called *maru*.

、 This marks a break in a sentence, much like the comma in English. Note the direction of the symbol. It goes from top left to bottom right. In Japanese this is called *ten*.

You may come across the following symbols when reading hiragana in authentic Japanese texts.

? This question mark is borrowed from English and typically used when the status of a sentence as a question is not clear due to the lack of the Japanese question marker /**ka**/ in informal speech.

! This exclamation mark is also borrowed from English.

The last two symbols have gained solid popularity in texting and other informal writing. However, they are not used in traditional writing and are still rare in official documents.

PART 1

Reading and Writing Writing Hiragana: The Basics

A Column

a

Aha! I caught a fish!

i

a flowing str**ea**m

u

I have the fl**u**

e

a bathing **e**lephant

o

surfing in the **o**cean

Writing Drill 1 🎧 Track 04

Read the samples, listen to the audio, and copy the words using the squares. Extra gridded paper for writing practice can be downloaded at the link on page 5.

ai love

あ い

ie house

い え

īe no

い い え

ao blue

あ お

ue above; on

う え

au meet

あ う

iu say

い う

Ka Column

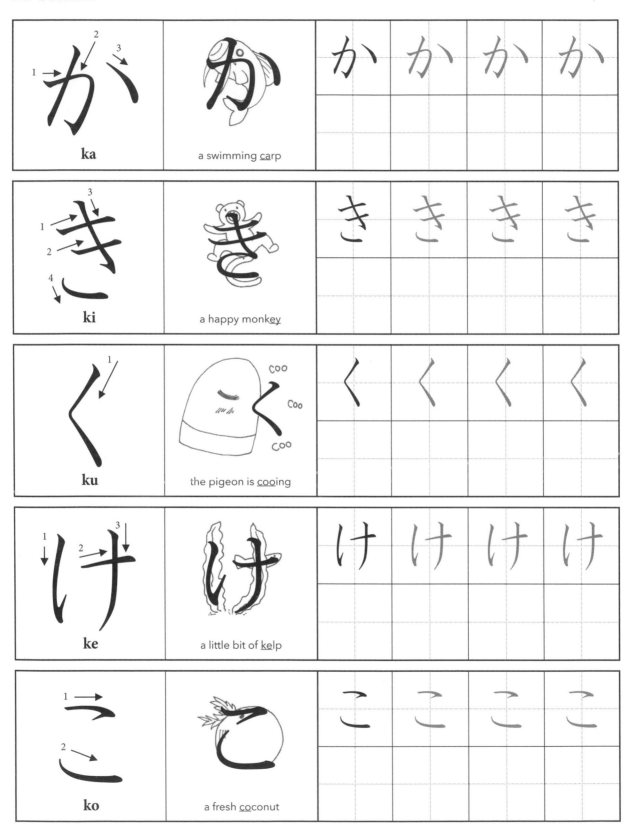

ka	a swimming <u>c</u>arp	か	か	か	か
ki	a happy mon<u>k</u>ey	き	き	き	き
ku	the pigeon is <u>coo</u>ing	く	く	く	く
ke	a little bit of <u>k</u>elp	け	け	け	け
ko	a fresh <u>co</u>conut	こ	こ	こ	こ

Ga Column

When two dots are added, /**k**/ becomes /**g**/.

が ga	が	が							
ぎ gi	ぎ	ぎ							
ぐ gu	ぐ	ぐ							
げ ge	げ	げ							
ご go	ご	ご							

Writing Drill 2 🎧 Track 05

Read the samples, listen to the audio, and copy the words using the squares.

aka red

あ	か												

kao face

か	お												

aki autumn

あ	き												

eki station

え	き												

kaki persimmon, oyster

か	き												

kiku listen; chrysanthemum

き く

iku go

い く

kega injury

け が

koko here

こ こ

koe voice

こ え

kagi key; lock

か ぎ

gogo afternoon

ご ご

koi koi carp; romantic love

こ い

eigo English

え い ご

kaigi meeting; conference

か い ぎ

eiga movie

え い が

keiko practice

け い こ

gaikoku foreign country

が い こ く

Sa Column

さ sa	try this <u>sau</u>ce	さ	さ	さ	さ
し shi	a grazing <u>shee</u>p	し	し	し	し
す su	I'm a <u>su</u>perhero!	す	す	す	す
せ se	<u>se</u>nd a letter	せ	せ	せ	せ
そ so	I'm <u>so</u> scared of snakes	そ	そ	そ	そ

Za Column

When two dots are added, unvoiced sounds become voiced.

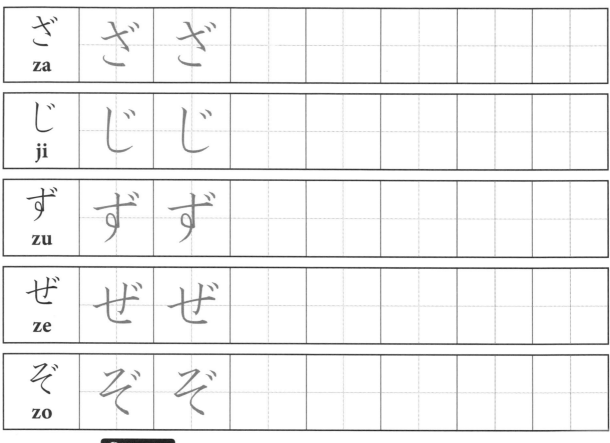

Writing Drill 3 🎧 Track 06

Read the samples, listen to the audio, and copy the words using the squares.

asa morning

| あ | さ | | | | | | | | | | | |

sushi sushi

| す | し | | | | | | | | | | | |

suzushī cool (temperature)

| す | ず | し | い | | | | | | | | | |

okashī funny, strange

| お | か | し | い | | | | | | | | | |

isu chair

| い | す | | | | | | | | | | | |

kasa umbrella
かさ

kesa this morning
けさ

sake sake; salmon
さけ

keizai economics
けいざい

okashi snack; sweets
おかし

soko there, in that place
そこ

asoko over there
あそこ

ashi leg; foot
あし

jiko accident
じこ

kaze wind; cold (sickness)
かぜ

kazoku family
かぞく

gakusei student
がくせい

seiji politics
せいじ

Ta Column

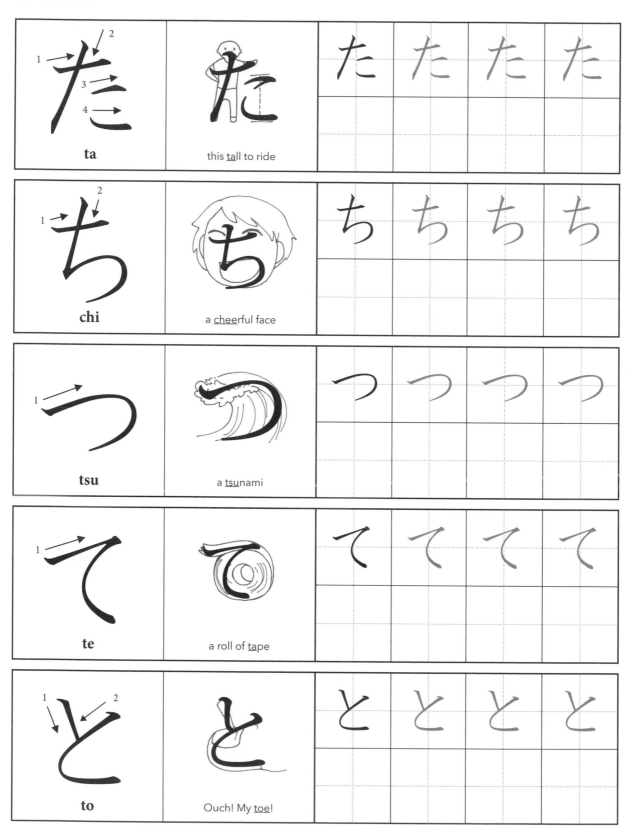

ta — this <u>ta</u>ll to ride

chi — a <u>chee</u>rful face

tsu — a <u>tsu</u>nami

te — a roll of <u>ta</u>pe

to — Ouch! My <u>toe</u>!

Da Column
When two dots are added, unvoiced sounds become voiced.

だ da	だ	だ							
ぢ ji	ぢ	ぢ							
づ zu	づ	づ							
で de	で	で							
ど do	ど	ど							

Writing Drill 4 🎧 Track 07
Read the samples, listen to the audio, and copy the words using the squares.

ashita tomorrow

| あ | し | た | | | | | | | | | | |

chichi (my) father

| ち | ち | | | | | | | | | | | |

otōto (my) young brother

| お | と | う | と | | | | | | | | | |

satō sugar

| さ | と | う | | | | | | | | | |

kutsu shoe

| く | つ | | | | | | | | | | |

kuchi mouth

く ち

tsukue desk

つ く え

chika basement

ち か

chikatetsu subway

ち か て つ

chizu map

ち ず

shigoto work

し ご と

utsu depression

う つ

tada free of charge; however

た だ

chīsai small

ち い さ い

doko where

ど こ

atode later

あ と で

dōshite why

ど う し て

tsuzuku to continue

つ づ く

ototoshi the year before last

おととし

uchi (my) home; inside

うち

otaku home; house (someone else's)

おたく

kita north; came

きた

soto outside

そと

katei home; family; household

かてい

take bamboo

たけ

atsui hot; thick

あつい

atatakai nice and warm

あたたかい

tatsu to stand

たつ

kisetsu season

きせつ

chikazuku to approach

ちかづく

shita below; did

した

Na Column

na	nautilus live in the ocean	な	な	な	な
ni	a needle and thread	に	に	に	に
nu	a very long noodle	ぬ	ぬ	ぬ	ぬ
ne	fishing with a net	ね	ね	ね	ね
no	Did you notice that?	の	の	の	の

Writing Drill 5 🎧 Track 08

Read the samples, listen to the audio, and copy the words using the squares.

nani what

| な | に | | | | | | | | | | |

inu dog

| い | ぬ | | | | | | | | | | |

neko cat

| ね | こ | | | | | | | | | | |

okane money

| お | か | ね | | | | | | | |

anata you

| あ | な | た | | | | | | | |

kinō yesterday

| き | の | う | | | | | | | |

niku meat

| に | く | | | | | | | | | | |

negi scallion; onion

| ね | ぎ | | | | | | | | | | |

sakana fish

| さ | か | な | | | | | | | |

nishi west

| に | し | | | | | | | | | | |

kanashī sad

| か | な | し | い | | | | | | |

shinu to die

| し | ぬ | | | | | | | | | | |

25

nanika something

なにか

naka inside; in

なか

natsukashī nostalgic

なつかしい

otonashī quiet, docile

おとなしい

toku ni particularly

とくに

tonikaku anyways; in any case

とにかく

nuno cloth

ぬの

kinu silk

きぬ

tanuki raccoon dog

たぬき

nai there is not; none; out of

ない

oishikunai not delicious

おいしくない

shitakunai do not want to do

したくない

dekinai cannot do

できない

Ha Column

は **ha**	that grave is <u>ha</u>unted	は	は	は	は
ひ **hi**	dogs can <u>he</u>ar very well	ひ	ひ	ひ	ひ
ふ **fu**	a cloud over Mt. <u>Fu</u>ji	ふ	ふ	ふ	ふ
へ **he**	a little <u>he</u>n	へ	へ	へ	へ
ほ **ho**	the hog is <u>ho</u>me	ほ	ほ	ほ	ほ

When two dots are added, /**h**/ becomes /**b**/.

ば **ba**	ば	ば						
び **bi**	び	び						
ぶ **bu**	ぶ	ぶ						
べ **be**	べ	べ						
ぼ **bo**	ぼ	ぼ						

When a small circle is added, /**h**/ becomes /**p**/.

ぱ **pa**	ぱ	ぱ						
ぴ **pi**	ぴ	ぴ						
ぷ **pu**	ぷ	ぷ						
ぺ **pe**	ぺ	ぺ						
ぽ **po**	ぽ	ぽ						

Writing Drill 6 🎧 Track 09

Read the samples, listen to the audio, and copy the words using the squares.

hai yes

| は | い | | | | | | | | | | | |

boku I (male; boy)

| ぼ | く | | | | | | | | | | | |

sofu (my) grandfather

| そ | ふ | | | | | | | | | | | |

sobo (my) grandmother

| そ | ぼ | | | | | | | | | | | |

higashi east

| ひ | が | し | | | | | | | |

hoshi star

| ほ | し | | | | | | | | | | | |

hako box

| は | こ | | | | | | | | | | | |

hito person

| ひ | と | | | | | | | | | | | |

heta poor at something

| へ | た | | | | | | | | | | | |

soba buckwheat noodle; nearby

| そ | ば | | | | | | | | | | | |

ebi shrimp

| え | び | | | | | | | | | | | |

tabun probably

| た | ぶ | ん | | | | | | | |

betsu separate

| べ | つ | | | | | | | | | |

Ma Column

ma

it's my grand<u>ma</u>

mi

meet a mum<u>my</u>

mu

<u>moo</u> says the cow

me

I won this <u>me</u>dal

mo

a <u>mo</u>torcycle

Writing Drill 7 🎧 Track 10

Read the samples, listen to the audio, and copy the words using the squares.

kimono kimono

き も の

tomodachi friend

と も だ ち

musume (my) daughter

む す め

musuko (my) son

む す こ

mago (my) grandchild

ま ご

atama head

あ た ま

sashimi sashimi

さ し み

osusume recommendation

お す す め

mise store; restaurant

み せ

migi right side

み ぎ

mado window

ま ど

minami south

み な み

Ya Column

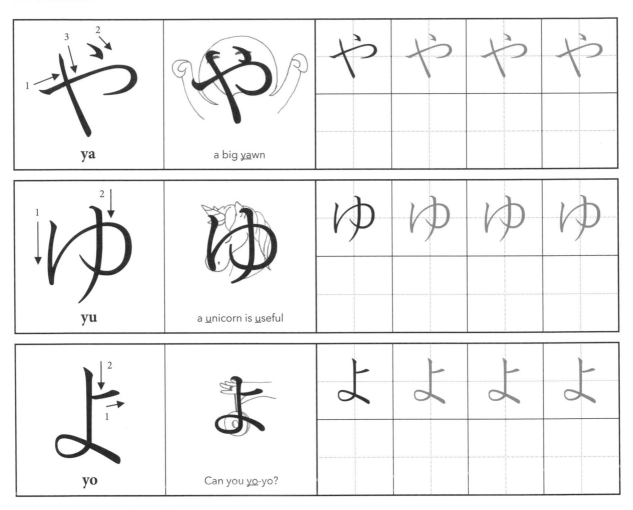

や **ya**	a big yawn	や	や	や	や
ゆ **yu**	a unicorn is useful	ゆ	ゆ	ゆ	ゆ
よ **yo**	Can you yo-yo?	よ	よ	よ	よ

Writing Drill 8 🎧 Track 11

Read the samples, listen to the audio, and copy the words using the squares.

iya no

い	や											

omiyage souvenir; gift

お	み	や	げ									

ohayō good morning

お	は	よ	う									

yōkoso welcome

よ	う	こ	そ									

oyasumi good night

おやすみ

nagoya Nagoya

なごや

fuyu winter

ふゆ

tsuyu rainy season

つゆ

yubi finger

ゆび

heya room

へや

yane roof

やね

yūbe last night

ゆうべ

yakusoku promise; appointment

やくそく

yasai vegetable

やさい

yuki snow

ゆき

yume dream

ゆめ

yoyaku reservation

よやく

Ra Column

ら **ra**	a zeb<u>ra</u> relaxing	ら	ら	ら	ら
り **ri**	tasty yakito<u>ri</u>	り	り	り	り
る **ru**	a mama kanga<u>roo</u>	る	る	る	る
れ **re**	<u>rest</u> in bed	れ	れ	れ	れ
ろ **ro**	bunnies in a bur<u>row</u>	ろ	ろ	ろ	ろ

Writing Drill 9 🎧 Track 12

Read the samples, listen to the audio, and copy the words using the squares.

dare who

だれ

kore this

これ

iriguchi entrance

いりぐち

futari two people

ふたり

karada body

からだ

haru spring

はる

hiru daytime; noon

ひる

onigiri rice ball

おにぎり

hiroi spacious; wide

ひろい

omoshiroi interesting

おもしろい

subarashī wonderful

すばらしい

ureshī happy; glad

うれしい

Wa Column

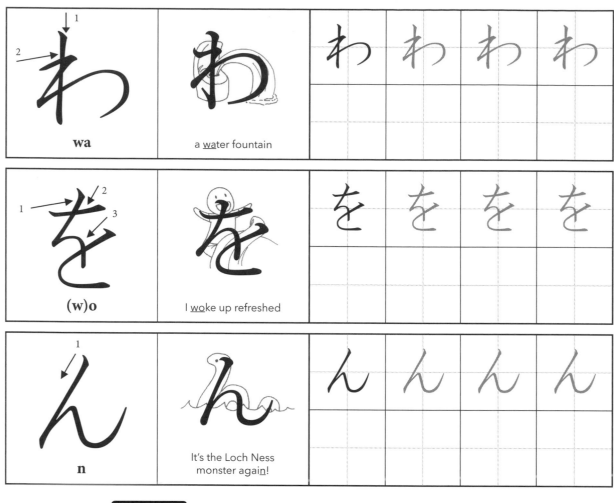

wa	a <u>wa</u>ter fountain	わ わ わ わ	
(w)o	I <u>wo</u>ke up refreshed	を を を を	
n	It's the Loch Ness monster ag<u>ain</u>!	ん ん ん ん	

Writing Drill 10   🎧 Track 13

Read the samples, listen to the audio, and copy the words using the squares.

watashi I, me

わ　た　し

sumimasen I'm sorry; excuse me

す　み　ま　せ　ん

gomen nasai I'm sorry (informal)

ご　め　ん　な　さ　い

renraku communication; contact

れ　ん　ら　く

unten drive

うんてん

wasabi wasabi

わさび

kawaī cute

かわいい

shiawase happy; happiness

しあわせ

okawari second serving

おかわり

gohan rice; meal

ごはん

udon udon noodles

うどん

tenpura tempura

てんぷら

tenki weather

てんき

hontō true; real

ほんとう

kowai scary; scared

こわい

shinbun o yomu read the newspaper

しんぶんをよむ

ringo o taberu eat an apple

りんごをたべる

Greetings and Common Expressions 🎧 Track 18

ohayō gozaimasu good morning (polite)

おはようございます

konnichiwa hello (daytime)

こんにちは

konbanwa good evening

こんばんは

dōzo please (offering something)

どうぞ

dōmo thank you (informal)

どうも

arigatō gozaimasu thank you (polite)

ありがとうございます

ieie no, no

いえいえ

dō itashimashite you are welcome

どういたしまして

tondemo arimasen not at all

とんでもありません

hajimemashite nice to meet you

はじめまして

onegai shimasu thank you in advance

おねがいします

sumimasen excuse me

すみません

gomen nasai I'm sorry (informal)

ご め ん な さ い

shitsurei shimasu excuse me; it's rude of me

し つ れ い し ま す

itadakimasu I'll start eating

い た だ き ま す

gochisōsama deshita thanks for the food/drink

ご ち そ う さ ま で し た

itte kimasu I'm going (and coming back later)

い っ て き ま す

itte rasshai see you when you come back

い っ て ら っ し ゃ い

tadaima I'm back (home)

た だ い ま

okaeri welcome back (informal)

お か え り

okaeri nasai welcome back (polite)

お か え り な さ い

sayonara goodbye

さ よ な ら

ki o tsukete safe trip; take care

き を つ け て

oyasumi nasai good night

お や す み な さ い

ja, mata see you; till next time

じ ゃ 、 ま た

Food and Drink

sushi sushi

す	し										

sakana fish

さ	か	な					

maguro tuna

ま	ぐ	ろ					

unagi eel

う	な	ぎ					

soba buckwheat noodles

そ	ば						

udon udon noodles

う	ど	ん					

gohan (cooked) rice; meal

ご	は	ん					

onigiri rice ball

お	に	ぎ	り				

tōfu tofu

と	う	ふ					

miso shiru miso soup

み	そ	し	る				

tamago egg

た	ま	ご					

tenpura tempura

て	ん	ぷ	ら				

yakitori skewered BBQ chicken

やきとり

kudamono fruit

くだもの

momo peach

もも

mikan mandarin orange

みかん

ringo apple

りんご

budō grape

ぶどう

yasai vegetable

やさい

jagaimo potato

じゃがいも

oyatsu snack

おやつ

okashi snack; sweet

おかし

taiyaki fish-shaped red bean cake

たいやき

shōyu soy sauce

しょうゆ

shio salt

しお

satō sugar
さとう

mizu water
みず

sake sake; salmon
さけ

kōcha black tea
こうちゃ

ocha tea; green tea
おちゃ

omakase chef's choice
おまかせ

okawari refill; seconds
おかわり

kanpai toast; cheers
かんぱい

otsumami snack to nibble while drinking
おつまみ

teishoku set meal
ていしょく

obentō bento; boxed meal
おべんとう

omochi kaeri take out
おもちかえり

kyō no osusume today's special
きょうのおすすめ

Reading and Writing Practice

I.   Circle the item that does not belong in each group. Check your answers on page 93.

Group A	Group B	Group C	Group D	Group E
ぶどう	ごはん	やきとり	すし	おすすめ
じゃがいも	うどん	おべんとう	しょうゆ	おはよう
りんご	おちゃ	かんぱい	さとう	おかわり
みかん	さかな	おにぎり	みそ	おまかせ
もも	おつまみ	とうふ	しお	おもちかえり

II.   Listen to audio track 21. Write down what you hear in hiragana. Answers are on page 93.

1. _____   6. _____

2. _____   7. _____

3. _____   8. _____

4. _____   9. _____

5. _____   10. _____

III. Listen to audio track 22. You are confirming lunch orders for your group. Write in hiragana what the following people want. Check your answers on page 93.

Ms. Suzuki   _____

Ms. Ito   _____

Teacher   _____

Mr. Johnson   _____

Mr. Tanaka   _____

IV. Which of the foods on pages 48–50 are your favorites? Make a list in hiragana.

People and Relationships 🎧 Track 23

watashi I, me

わ　た　し

ore I, me (male, informal)

お　れ

hito person

ひ　と

kare he; boyfriend

か　れ

kanojo she; girlfriend

か　の　じ　ょ

minasan everyone (polite)

み　な　さ　ん

otona adult

お　と　な

kodomo child

こ　ど　も

okāsan mother

お　か　あ　さ　ん

otōsan father

お　と　う　さ　ん

onēsan big sister

お　ね　え　さ　ん

onīsan big brother

お　に　い　さ　ん

ane my big sister

あ ね

ani my big brother

あ に

imōto my little sister

い も う と

otōto my little brother

お と う と

musume daughter

む す め

musuko son

む す こ

oya parent

お や

kyōdai siblings

き ょ う だ い

mei niece

め い

oi nephew

お い

itoko cousin

い と こ

oba aunt

お ば

oji uncle

お じ

tomodachi friend

と　も　だ　ち

gaikokujin foreigner

が　い　こ　く　じ　ん

motokano ex-girlfriend

も　と　か　の

motokare ex-boyfriend

も　と　か　れ

senpai senior in the group

せ　ん　ぱ　い

kōhai junior in the group

こ　う　は　い

buka subordinate

ぶ　か

jōshi boss; supervisor

じ　ょ　う　し

shachō president of company

し　ゃ　ち　ょ　う

buchō division chief

ぶ　ち　ょ　う

omawarisan police officer

お　ま　わ　り　さ　ん

isha doctor

い　し　ゃ

sensei teacher

せ　ん　せ　い

Reading and Writing Practice

I.   Circle the item that does not belong in each group. Check your answers on page 93.

Group A	Group B	Group C	Group D	Group E
あね	あに	もとかれ	めい	おば
ぶちょう	ぶか	おじさん	うんてんしゅ	おじ
いもうと	こうはい	おい	しゃちょう	おい
おとうさん	じょうし	おれ	せんせい	おや
おかあさん	せんぱい	かのじょ	いしゃ	おちゃ

II. Listen to audio track 24. Write down what you hear in hiragana. Answers are on page 93.

1. _____   6. _____

2. _____   7. _____

3. _____   8. _____

4. _____   9. _____

5. _____   10. _____

III. Listen to audio track 25. Identify who that person (*ano hito*) is. Write the answers in hiragana. Check your answers on page 93.

1. あのひとは_____です。

2. あのひとは_____です。

3. あのひとは_____です。

4. あのひとは_____です。

5. あのひとは_____です。

IV. Make a list of the members of your family, using hiragana.

Part 2

muzukashī difficult

むずかしい

yasashī easy; kind

やさしい

majime serious

まじめ

kirei pretty; clean

きれい

shinsetsu kind

しんせつ

dame useless

だめ

ureshī happy

うれしい

kanashī sad

かなしい

hiroi wide, spacious

ひろい

semai narrow, small

せまい

atarashī new

あたらしい

furui old

ふるい

hikui low

ひくい

58

Reading and Writing Practice

I. Draw a line to connect each adjective to its opposite meaning. Check your answers on page 93.

1. よわい	a) かなしい
2. やわらかい	b) ひくい
3. くらい	c) わるい
4. ちかい	d) つよい
5. うれしい	e) あつい
6. たかい	f) とおい
7. さむい	g) すくない
8. うるさい	h) しずか
9. おおい	i) かたい
10. いい	j) あかるい

II. Listen to audio track 27. Fill the blanks with the words you hear in hiragana. Check your answers on page 94.

1. _____ ひと

2. _____ せんせい

3. _____ すし

4. _____ な　おねえさん

5. _____ くだもの

6. _____ さけ

7. _____ な　いしゃ

8. _____ おとうさん

9. _____ みかん

10. _____ な　ぶか

III. Fill the blank with the word that has the opposite meaning. Answers are on page 94.

おおい	おいしい	せまい	ちかい	ながい	おおきい

IV. Write a list of adjectives to describe your best friend, your boss, and yourself. How about your job, school, house or apartment?

Questions, Requests and Responses 🎧 Track 28

nan desu ka what is (it)?

なんですか

dare desu ka who is (it)?

だれですか

itsu desu ka when is (it)?

いつですか

doko desu ka where is (it)?

どこですか

dōshite why

どうして

dore desu ka which one is (it)?

どれですか

ikura desu ka how much is (it)?

いくらですか

kudasai please give (it) to me

ください

onegai shimasu I humbly request (it)

おねがいします

chōdai give (it) to me (informal)

ちょうだい

kure give (it) to me (informal; rough)

くれ

hai that's right; here I am; here you are

はい

ē that's right (less formal)

| え | え | | | | | | | | | | | | |

un that's right (informal)

| う | ん | | | | | | | | | | | | |

īe that's wrong; no

| い | い | え | | | | | | | | | |

iya that's wrong; well

| い | や | | | | | | | | | | | | |

uun that's wrong (informal)

| う | う | ん | | | | | | | | |

kore this

| こ | れ | | | | | | | | | | | | |

sore that (near the addressee)

| そ | れ | | | | | | | | | | | | |

are that (away from both speakers)

| あ | れ | | | | | | | | | | | | |

koko here

| こ | こ | | | | | | | | | | | | |

soko there (where the addressee is)

| そ | こ | | | | | | | | | | | | |

asoko over there

| あ | そ | こ | | | | | | | | | |

kono this

| こ | の | | | | | | | | | | | | |

sono that

| そ | の | | | | | | | | | | | | |

ano   that over there

あ の

takusan   a lot

た く さ ん

zenzen   never

ぜ ん ぜ ん

itsumo   always

い つ も

mainichi   every day

ま い に ち

tokidoki   sometimes

と き ど き

tama ni   every now and then

た ま に

chotto   a little bit

ち ょ っ と

sukoshi   a little bit (formal)

す こ し

totemo   very

と て も

yoku   often; very well

よ く

mecha   very (colloquial)

め ちゃ

chō   super (colloquial)

ち ょ う

Reading and Writing Practice

I. Fill in the blank with the most appropriate phrase. Check your answers on page 94.

1. You want to know what this package is. これ、＿＿＿＿＿＿＿＿＿＿＿＿＿＿＿＿。
   a) どこですか。 　　　　　 b) だれですか。 　　 c) なんですか。

2. A friend will be late. Ask him why. ＿＿＿＿＿＿＿＿＿＿＿＿＿＿＿＿＿＿。
   a) なんで？ 　　　　　 b) なぜですか。 　　 c) どれ？

3. Ask the shopkeeper to give you this item (near to you). ＿＿＿＿＿＿＿＿＿ください。
   a) あれ 　　　　　 b) それ 　　　　　 c) これ

4. Ask the shopkeeper to give you that item (near to the shopkeeper). ＿＿＿＿＿ください。
   a) あれ 　　　　　 b) それ 　　　　　 c) これ

5. Ask the shopkeeper to give you that item over there (far from both of you).
   ＿＿＿＿＿ください。

   a) あれ 　　　　　 b) それ 　　　　　 c) これ

II. Listen to audio track 29. Fill the blanks with the words you hear in hiragana. Check your answers on page 94.

1. ＿＿＿＿＿＿＿＿＿＿＿ ですか。　6. ＿＿＿＿＿＿＿＿＿＿ だめです。

2. あれ、＿＿＿＿ ＿＿＿＿ ですか。　7. りんご、＿＿＿＿＿ おねがいします。

3. これ、＿＿＿＿＿＿＿＿＿。　8. このすし、＿＿＿＿＿＿ おいしい。

4. ＿＿＿＿＿＿＿＿＿、どうぞ。　9. ＿＿＿＿＿＿＿＿＿、すみません。

5. そのおべんとう、＿＿＿＿ ですか。　10. ちょっと、＿＿＿＿＿＿＿＿＿。

III. Write a hiragana word to say how often you do the following:

1. Take a walk ＿＿＿＿＿＿＿＿＿　5. Eat Japanese food ＿＿＿＿＿＿＿

2. Watch TV ＿＿＿＿＿＿＿＿＿　6. Drink beer ＿＿＿＿＿＿＿＿＿

3. Tweet ＿＿＿＿＿＿＿＿＿　7. Drive a car ＿＿＿＿＿＿＿＿＿

4. Exercise ＿＿＿＿＿＿＿＿＿　8. Yoga ＿＿＿＿＿＿＿＿＿

senshū last week

せ ん し ゅ う

kongetsu this month

こ ん げ つ

raigetsu next month

ら い げ つ

sengetsu last month

せ ん げ つ

kotoshi this year

こ と し

rainen next year

ら い ね ん

kyonen last year

き ょ ね ん

tanjōbi birthday

た ん じ ょ う び

haru spring

は る

natsu summer

な つ

aki fall

あ き

fuyu winter

ふ ゆ

tsuyu rainy season

つ ゆ

Reading and Writing Practice

I.   Circle the item that does not belong in each group. Check your answers on page 94.

Group A	Group B	Group C	Group D	Group E
きのう	ことし	なつ	いつ	あした
きょねん	あさって	たんじょうび	なんじ	あそこ
せんしゅう	きょう	ふゆ	どうして	あね
せんげつ	けさ	あき	どこ	あかるい
らいねん	こんしゅう	はる	かようび	あまい

II.   Fill in the blank with the most appropriate word. Check your answers on page 94.

1. Find out what time it is. いま、_____ですか。
    a) いつ   b) なんじ   c) なんじかん

2. Tell everyone it's time. _____です。
    a) じかん   b) あさ   c) いま

3. Tell everyone the meeting (*kaigi*) is this week. かいぎは_____です。
    a) こんしゅう   b) こんげつ   c) ことし

4. Exclaim how early 7:00am is (for the meeting). _____7じは、はやいですねえ。
    a) あさ   b) ごご   c) ばん

5. Exclaim it's Friday (TGIF)! _____ですねえ！
    a) しゅうまつ   b) にちようび   c) きんようび

6. Say your birthday was the day before yesterday. たんじょうび、_____でした。
    a) あさって   b) おととい   c) おととし

7. Tell a visitor it's the rainy season now. いま_____です。
    a) なつ   b) ふゆ   c) つゆ

8. Say the store is closed (*yasumi*) on Monday. このみせは、_____は、やすみです。
    a) こんげつ   b) げつようび   c) ゆうべ

III.   Which season do you like most? Which day of the week do you like most? What time do
     you usually get up? What time do you usually go to bed? Write the times using the Arabic
     number and hiragana.

Verbs

shimasu to do

し	ま	す						

imasu to be (people, animals)

い	ま	す						

arimasu to be (things)

あ	り	ま	す					

irimasu to need

い	り	ま	す					

dekimasu can

で	き	ま	す					

wakarimasu to understand

わ	か	り	ま	す				

nemasu to sleep

ね	ま	す						

okimasu to wake up

お	き	ま	す					

mimasu to look

み	ま	す						

kakimasu to write

か	き	ま	す					

yomimasu to read

よ	み	ま	す					

kikimasu to listen; ask

き	き	ま	す					

tabemasu to eat

たべます

nomimasu to drink

のみます

kaimasu to buy

かいます

ikimasu to go

いきます

kimasu to come

きます

kaerimasu to return

かえります

machimasu to wait

まちます

hatarakimasu to work

はたらきます

benkyō shimasu to study

べんきょうします

tsukemasu to switch on

つけます

keshimasu to switch off

けします

ganbarimasu to do one's best

がんばります

tsukurimasu to make

つくります

tsukaimasu to use

つ か い ま す

aimasu to meet

あ い ま す

asobimasu to play

あ そ び ま す

haraimasu to pay

は ら い ま す

dekakemasu to go out

で か け ま す

waraimasu to laugh

わ ら い ま す

nakimasu to cry

な き ま す

okorimasu to get angry

お こ り ま す

homemasu to praise

ほ め ま す

shikarimasu to scold

し か り ま す

yukkuri shimasu to relax

ゆ っ く り し ま す

gakkari shimasu to be disappointed

が っ か り し ま す

bikkuri shimasu to be surprised

び っ く り し ま す

Reading and Writing Practice

I.   Fill in the blank with the most appropriate word. Check your answers on page 94.

1. Ask if a coworker understand this. これ、＿＿＿＿＿＿＿＿＿＿＿＿＿か。
    a) わかります　　　　　　b) します　　　　　c) できます

2. Let a coworker know that you will take tomorrow off. あした ＿＿＿＿＿＿＿＿＿＿。
    a) やすみます　　　　　　b) でかけます　　　c) はたらきます

3. An important deadline is near. Tell your boss that you'll do your best. ＿＿＿＿＿＿＿＿。
    a) できます　　　　　　　b) がんばります　　c) します

4. Tell a coworker that you are going home. ＿＿＿＿＿＿＿＿＿＿＿。
    a) いきます　　　　　　　b) かえります　　　c) きます

5. At the end of a meal at a restaurant, offer to pay for everyone. わたしが ＿＿＿＿＿＿。
    a) はらいます　　　　　　b) わらいます　　　c) のみます

6. Tell a coworker that you are meeting a friend. ともだちに＿＿＿＿＿＿＿。
    a) あります　　　　　　　b) あいます　　　　c) あそびます

7. Mention that you will study on weekends. しゅうまつは、べんきょう＿＿＿＿＿。
    a) います　　　　　　　　b) いります　　　　c) します

8. Mention that your boss often gets angry. じょうしは、よく＿＿＿＿＿＿＿＿＿。
    a) おこります　　　　　　b) おきます　　　　c) なきます

9. Ask a friend if he makes bento every day. まいにち、おべんとうを＿＿＿＿＿か。
    a) つかいます　　　　　　b) つくります　　　c) かいます

II. Listen to the daily routine described in audio track 32. Fill in the blanks in hiragana. Check your answers on page 94.

1. 6:00   ＿＿＿＿＿＿＿＿＿＿＿。　　6. 3:00   かいぎに＿＿＿＿＿＿＿。

2. 7:00   あさごはんを＿＿＿＿＿。　　7. 6:00   ともだちと＿＿＿＿＿＿。

3. 8:00   かいしゃに＿＿＿＿＿＿。　　8. 9:00   いえに＿＿＿＿＿＿＿＿。

4. 9:00   しごとを＿＿＿＿＿＿＿。　　9. 10:00 ＿＿＿＿＿＿＿＿＿＿。

5. 12:00 おべんとうを＿＿＿＿＿。　　10. 11:00 ＿＿＿＿＿＿＿＿＿＿。

III. Read each context. Respond orally first, and then write a simple note in hiragana. Compare your ideas with the sample answers on page 94.

1. Tell a coworker that you work weekends.
2. Tell a coworker that you are going home.
3. Ask a coworker if he understands this.
4. Tell a coworker that you will go out today.
5. A coworker is wondering when a package will come. Tell him it will come tomorrow.

IV. Using exercise II as a model, list your daily activities and the time they take place.

umi sea; ocean

うみ

shima island

しま

kawa river

かわ

michi road; street

みち

hashi bridge

はし

kōsaten intersection

こうさてん

kuruma car

くるま

hikōki airplane

ひこうき

fune boat; ship

ふね

jitensha bicycle

じてんしゃ

densha train

でんしゃ

shinkansen bullet train

しんかんせん

chikatetsu subway

ちかてつ

Reading and Writing Practice

I. Draw a line between the hiragana word and its reading in English. Check your answers on page 94.

1.	おおさか	a)	Fukushima
2.	おきなわ	b)	Akihabara
3.	ひろしま	c)	Hokkaido
4.	あきはばら	d)	Osaka
5.	きゅうしゅう	e)	Kyoto
6.	きょうと	f)	Yokohama
7.	よこはま	g)	Kyushu
8.	ほっかいどう	h)	Okinawa
9.	ふくしま	i)	Hiroshima
10.	はらじゅく	j)	Harajuku

II. Listen to audio track 34 and write in hiragana where the person is going. Check your answers on page 94.

1. _____   6. _____

2. _____   7. _____

3. _____   8. _____

4. _____   9. _____

5. _____   10. _____

III. Fill in the blanks in hiragana. Check your answers on page 95.

1. I'm going to Ueno by train. _____ に _____ でいきます。
2. I'm going to Nagoya by train. _____ に _____ でいきます。
3. I'm going to Kyoto by bullet train. _____ に _____ でいきます。
4. I'm going to Narita Airport by subway. _____ に _____ でいきます。
5. I'm going to the countryside by car. _____ に _____ でいきます。
6. I'm going to school by bicycle. _____ に _____ でいきます。
7. I'm going to Okinawa by plane. _____ に _____ でいきます。
8. I'm going to the island by boat. _____ に _____ でいきます。
9. I'm going to Mt. Fuji by car. _____ に _____ でいきます。
10. I'm going to the river by bicycle. _____ に _____ でいきます。

IV. List the places you have visited, or would like to visit in Japan. If their names are not included in this section, do an online search.

Education

kyōiku education

| き | ょ | う | い | く | | | | | | | | | | | | | |

gakkō school

| が | っ | こ | う | | | | | | | | | | | | | |

hoikuen nursery school

| ほ | い | く | え | ん | | | | | | | | | | | | | |

yōchien kindergarten

| よ | う | ち | え | ん | | | | | | | | | | | | | |

shōgakkō elementary school

| し | ょ | う | が | っ | こ | う | | | | | | | | |

chūgakkō middle school

| ち | ゅ | う | が | っ | こ | う | | | | | | | | |

kōkō high school

| こ | う | こ | う | | | | | | | | | | | | | |

daigaku university; college

| だ | い | が | く | | | | | | | | | | | | | |

tōdai Tokyo University

| と | う | だ | い | | | | | | | | | | | | | |

kyōdai Kyoto University

| き | ょ | う | だ | い | | | | | | | | | | | | | |

juku cram school

| じ | ゅ | く | | | | | | | | | | | | | |

kyōshitsu classroom

| き | ょ | う | し | つ | | | | | | | | | | | | | |

kyōkasho textbook

きょうかしょ

enpitsu pencil

えんぴつ

keshigomu eraser

けしごむ

jugyō lesson

じゅぎょう

shukudai homework

しゅくだい

shiken exam

しけん

seiseki grade

せいせき

sotsugyō graduation

そつぎょう

juken taking entrance exam

じゅけん

gōkaku passing an exam

ごうかく

gakusei student

がくせい

seito pupil

せいと

kokugo Japanese for native speakers

こくご

eigo English

えいご

sūgaku mathematics

すうがく

tai-iku PE

たいいく

ongaku music

おんがく

rekishi history

れきし

keizai economics

けいざい

seiji politics

せいじ

butsuri physics

ぶつり

kagaku chemistry; science

かがく

bungaku literature

ぶんがく

eibungaku English literature

えいぶんがく

ryūgaku study abroad

りゅうがく

kenkyū research

けんきゅう

Reading and Writing Practice

I.   Circle the item that does not belong in each group. Check your answers on page 95.

Group A	Group B	Group C	Group D	Group E
がくせい	れきし	せいと	えいご	いえ
じゅく	けいざい	じゅぎょう	きょうかしょ	くうこう
こうこう	せいじ	けんきゅう	こくご	えんぴつ
だいがく	ぶんがく	べんきょう	すうがく	がっこう
しょうがっこう	せいと	しけん	ぶつり	ようちえん

II. Listen to audio track 36. Write the words you hear in hiragana. Check your answers on page 95.

1. _____   6. _____

2. _____   7. _____

3. _____   8. _____

4. _____   9. _____

5. _____   10. _____

III. Listen to audio track 37. Make a note in hiragana of who each person is and their educational background or current status. Check your answers on page 95.

Person	Background
1.	
2.	
3.	
4.	
5.	

IV. Make a list of your favorite school subjects, using hiragana.

kimono kimono

き	も	の											

yukata casual cotton kimono

ゆ	か	た											

geta wooden flipflops

げ	た													

yakimono ceramics; pottery

や	き	も	の										

nurimono lacquer ware

ぬ	り	も	の										

urushi Japanese lacquer

う	る	し											

haiku haiku poetry

は	い	く											

yakyū baseball

や	き	ゅ	う										

manga manga; comic strip

ま	ん	が											

omatsuri festival

お	ま	つ	り										

onsen hot spring

お	ん	せ	ん										

hanami flower viewing

は	な	み											

hanabi fireworks

は	な	び											

Reading and Writing Practice

I.   Circle the item that does not belong in each group. Check your answers on page 95.

Group A	Group B	Group C	Group D	Group E
おしろ	こと	あいきどう	おまつり	しょうぎ
おてら	ぶんか	すもう	はなみ	さどう
はいく	げた	やきゅう	かぶき	おんせん
びょういん	たいこ	じゅうどう	ざぜん	けんどう
がっこう	きもの	からて	じんじゃ	ぼんさい

II.   Listen to audio track 41. Write the words you hear in hiragana. Check your answers on page 95.

1. _____   6. _____

2. _____   7. _____

3. _____   8. _____

4. _____   9. _____

5. _____   10. _____

III. You have been asked what you like (*suki desu*) about Japan. Fill each blank in hiragana. Check your answers on page 95.

1. I like sumo. _____が、すきです。

2. I like flower arrangement and tea ceremony. _____と_____がすきです。

3. I like judo and karate. _____と_____がすきです。

4. I like shrines and temples. _____と_____がすきです。

5. I like kimono and Japanese dance. _____と_____がすきです。

IV. Using exercise III as a model, write sentences about which cultural activities you like.

izonshō addiction

いぞんしょう

jisatsu suicide

じさつ

dōseikon same sex marriage

どうせいこん

chikyū ondanka global warming

ちきゅうおんだんか

kankyō environment

かんきょう

jizoku kanō sustainable

じぞくかのう

bōsai disaster prevention

ぼうさい

genpatsu nuclear power plant

げんぱつ

sagi fraud

さぎ

kaigo care for the elderly

かいご

hatarakikata work practice

はたらきかた

netchūshō heatstroke

ねっちゅうしょう

kosodate child-rearing

こそだて

josei shinshutsu advancement of women

じょせいしんしゅつ

taiki jidō child on waiting list for child care

たいきじどう

genkai shūraku depopulated village, mostly with seniors

げんかいしゅうらく

fukkō (economic) recovery

ふっこう

mottai nai it's a waste; too good

もったいない

sansei shimasu to agree; to approve

さんせいします

hantai shimasu to oppose; to disapprove

はんたいします

okimasu to arise; to happen

おきます

fuemasu to increase

ふえます

herimasu to decrease

へります

susumimasu to advance; to continue

すすみます

hidoku narimasu to get worse; to get terrible

ひどくなります

yoku narimasu to get better; to recover

よくなります

Reading and Writing Practice

I.   Circle the item that does not belong in each group. Check your answers on page 95.

Group A	Group B	Group C	Group D	Group E
ねんきん	どうせいこん	さべつ	うつ	しょうしか
はけん	にんちしょう	ぎゃくたい	じさつ	はけん
いみん	いぞんしょう	いじめ	ひきこもり	かそか
せんせい	うつ	かんきょう	ふとうこう	こうれいか
せいと	がん	かていないぼうりょく	げんぱつ	おんだんか

II. Listen to the problems (*mondai*) on audio track 43 and then write them in hiragana. Check your answers on page 96.

1. _____   6. _____

2. _____   7. _____

3. _____   8. _____

4. _____   9. _____

5. _____   10. _____

III. Fill in the name of the problem (*mondai*) in hiragana. Check your answers on page 96.

1. The problem is global warming.   もんだいは、_____です。

2. The problem is domestic violence.   もんだいは、_____です。

3. The problem is child abuse.   もんだいは、こどもの_____です。

4. The problems are bullying and truancy.   もんだいは、_____と_____です。

5. The problems are depression and suicide. もんだいは、_____と_____です。

IV. Make a list in hiragana of the issues mentioned in this section that you are most concerned about, in order of importance.

Answer Key

Page 47, I:

1. c   2. a   3. c   4. a   5. c   6. a   7. c

Page 47, II Audio Script:

1. ごちそうさまでした。
2. がんばってください。
3. おめでとう。
4. おはようございます。
5. いらっしゃいませ。
6. さようなら。
7. どうぞごゆっくり。
8. おやすみなさい。
9. ありがとうございます。
10. どういたしまして。

Page 47, III: Sample answers:

1. おはようございます。
2. いってきます。
3. どうぞ。
4. いらっしゃいませ。
5. おさきに。

Page 51, I:

Group A じゃがいも   Group B おちゃ   Group C かんぱい   Group D すし   Group E おはよう

Page 51, II Audio Script:

1. うどん
2. りんごとみかん
3. とうふのみそしる
4. やさいとくだもの
5. さけのおつまみ
6. おちゃとおかし
7. やきとりべんとう
8. きょうのおすすめ
9. ごはんのおかわり
10. さけのおにぎり

Page 51, III Audio Script:

1. すずきさんは、やきとりべんとうとおちゃです。
2. いとうさんは、さけのおにぎりとりんごです。
3. せんせいは、きょうのおすすめのてんぷらうどんです。
4. ジョンソンさんは、すしのおまかせです。
5. たなかさんは、さかなのていしょくです。

Page 55, I:

Group A ぶちょう   Group B あに   Group C かのじ   Group D めい   Group E おちゃ

Page 55, II Audio Script:

1. かれのおべんとう
2. わたしのせんせい
3. がいこくじんのともだち
4. おかあさん、おはよう。
5. みなさん、おはようございます。
6. おかあさん、おとうさん、いってきます。
7. かれのかのじょ
8. もとかののおかあさん
9. せんぱいのめい
10. わたしのおすすめ

Page 55, III Audio Script:

1. あのひとは、ともだちのおかあさんです。
2. あのひとは、いもうとのもとかれです。
3. あのひとは、がいこくじんのともだちです。
4. あのひとは、うちのしゃちょうのこうはいです。
5. あのひとは、せんぱいのおねえさんです。

Page 59, I:

1. d   2. i   3. j   4. f   5. a   6. b   7. e   8. h   9. g   10. c

Page 59, II Audio Script:

1. いいひと
2. あたらしいせんせい
3. おいしいすし
4. きれいなおねえさん
5. やわらかいくだもの
6. つよいさけ
7. だめないしゃ
8. やさしいおとうさん
9. やすいみかん
10. まじめなぶか

Page 59, III:

おおい	おいしい	せまい	ちかい	ながい	おおきい
すくない	まずい	ひろい	とおい	みじかい	ちいさい

Page 63, I:

1. c　　2. a　　3. c　　4. b　　5. a

Page 63, II:

1. どうしてですか。
2. あれ、いつですか。
3. これ、ください。
4. たくさん、どうぞ。
5. そのおべんとう、いくらですか。
6. いえいえ、だめです。
7. りんご、すこしおねがいします。
8. このすし、めちゃおいしい。
9. いつも、すみません。
10. ちょっと、ちょうだい。

Page 67, I:

Group A らいねん　　Group B あさって　　Group C たんじょうび　　Group D かようび　　Group E あした

Page 67, II:

1. b　　2. a　　3. a　　4. a　　5. c　　6. b　　7. c　　8 b.

Page 71, I:

1. a　　2. a　　3. b　　4. b　　5. a　　6. b　　7. c　　8. a　　9. a　　10. b

Page 71, II Audio Script:

1. 6じにおきます。
2. 7じにあさごはんをたべます。
3. 8じにかいしゃにいきます。
4. 9じにしごとをします。
5. 12じにおべんとうをかいます。
6. 3じにかいぎにいきます。
7. 6じにともだちとあいます。
8. 9じにいえにかえります。
9. 10じにべんきょうします。
10. 11じにねます。

Page 71, III. Sample answers:

1. しゅうまつ、はたらきます。
2. かえります。
3. わかりますか。
4. きょう、でかけます。
5. あした、きます。

Page 75, I:

1. d　　2. h　　3. i　　4. b　　5. g　　6. e　　7. f　　8. c　　9. a　　10. j

Page 75, II Audio Script:

1. うみにいきます。
2. きょうとにいきます。
3. いなかにいきます。
4. ほっかいどうにいきます。
5. ぎんざにいきます。
6. こうさてんにいきます。
7. きゅうしゅうのしまにいきます。
8. よこはまのみなとにいきます。
9. なりたくうこうにいきます。
10. しこくのかわにいきます。

Page 75, III:
1. うえのにでんしゃでいきます。
2. なごやにでんしゃでいきます。
3. きょうとにしんかんせんでいきます。
4. なりたくうこうにちかてつでいきます。
5. いなかにくるまでいきます。
6. がっこうにじてんしゃでいきます。
7. おきなわにひこうきでいきます。
8. しまにふねでいきます。
9. ふじさんにともだちのくるまでいきます。
10. かわにじてんしゃでいきます。

Page 79, I:
Group A がくせい　Group B せいと　Group C せいと　Group D きょうかしょ　Group E えんぴつ

Page 79, II Audio Script:
1. しゅくだい
2. えいご
3. しけん
4. せいせき
5. ぶつり
6. すうがく
7. じゅけん
8. そつぎょう
9. りゅうがく
10. けしごむ

Page 79, III Audio Script:
1. むすめは、しょうがっこうです。
2. おかあさんは、とうだいです。
3. あには、すうがくのせんせいです。
4. いもうとは、ちゅうがっこうです。
5. あねのけんきゅうは、ぶつりです。

Page 83, I:
Group A しんぞう　Group B あし　Group C くすり　Group D すね　Group E しょうじょう

Page 83, II Audio Script:
1. のど
2. め
3. あし
4. みみ

Page 83, III:
1. け
2. あたま
3. みみ
4. はな
5. め
6. くち
7. ゆび
8. て
9. うで
10. あし

Page 87, I:
Group A はいく　Group B ぶんか　Group C やきゅう　Group D じんじゃ　Group E おんせん

Page 87, II Audio Script:
1. おんせん
2. ぼんさい
3. きもの
4. いけばな
5. おまつり
6. すもう
7. おしろ
8. でんとうとぶんか
9. ぶっきょうとしんとう
10. おてらとじんじゃ

Page 87, III:
1. すもう
2. いけばな、さどう
3. じゅうどう、からて
4. じんじゃ、おてら
5. きもの、にほんぶよう

Page 92, I:
Group A ねんきん　Group B どうせいこん　Group C かんきょう　Group D げんぱつ　Group E はけん

Page 92, II Audio Script:

1. もんだいはかくさです。
2. もんだいはげんぱつです。
3. もんだいはいじめです。
4. もんだいはかいごです。
5. もんだいはしょうしかです。

6. もんだいはおれおれさぎです。
7. もんだいはひんこんです。
8. もんだいはじさつです。
9. もんだいはかていないぼうりょくです。
10. もんだいはちきゅうおんだんかです。

Page 92, III:

1. ちきゅうおんだんか
2. かていないぼうりょく
3. ぎゃくたい
4. いじめ、ふとうこう
5. うつ、じさつ